OnlyFans Unlocked

OnlyFans Unlocked

Valentina Reid

CONTENTS

Introduction to OnlyFans

Understanding the OnlyFans Platform

Understanding the OnlyFans platform requires a comprehensive grasp of its functionalities and how they cater to content creators. Launched in 2016, OnlyFans has quickly become a popular venue for various types of creators, including models, influencers, and adult entertainers. It allows users to monetize their content through subscriptions, offering a direct way to connect with fans. The platform operates on a subscription-based model, which means that creators charge their subscribers a monthly fee to access exclusive content.

This creates a sustainable income stream for those who effectively engage their audience.

Content creation strategies on OnlyFans are pivotal for success. Unlike traditional social media platforms, OnlyFans encourages a more intimate connection with subscribers, allowing creators to share content that is often more personal or exclusive. This can include behind-the-scenes content, tutorials, or personalized messages. Models and creators need to identify what unique offerings they can provide to attract and retain subscribers. High-quality content that resonates with the audience is essential, as it not only justifies the subscription fee but also fosters loyalty and encourages word-of-mouth promotion.

Marketing techniques are crucial for gaining visibility on OnlyFans. Social media platforms like Twitter, Instagram, and TikTok can be powerful tools for driving traffic to an OnlyFans account. Creators should leverage these platforms to showcase snippets of their content, engage with potential subscribers, and build a personal brand. Collaborations with other creators can also enhance visibility and attract new audiences. In addition, understanding SEO strategies to optimize profiles and posts can significantly impact discoverability, allowing creators to reach a wider audience more effectively.

Beyond the subscription model, monetization methods on OnlyFans can significantly enhance income. Creators can offer pay-per-view content, tips, and exclusive one-on-one interactions. Bundling services or creating tiered subscription levels can also provide additional revenue streams. Moreover, utilizing merchandise or affiliate marketing can diversify income and attract a broader audience. Understanding various monetization strategies allows creators to maximize their earning potential while maintaining a loyal subscriber base.

Building an engaged community is vital for long-term success on OnlyFans. Interaction with subscribers through personalized content, responding to messages, and hosting live sessions can create a sense of belonging and loyalty. It's important for creators to cultivate a brand identity that resonates with their audience, ensuring that their personal values and aesthetic align with their content. Legal considerations, including understanding the platform's regulations and local laws regarding adult content, are equally important. A solid foundation in these areas will enable creators to navigate the complexities of the industry while building a sustainable and profitable business.

The Evolution of Content Creation

The landscape of content creation has evolved dramatically over the past few decades, particularly with the advent of digital platforms. Initially, content creation was largely limited to traditional media, with artists, writers, and performers relying on gatekeepers such as publishers, record labels, and television networks to distribute their work. This model often restricted access for many aspiring creators, who found it challenging to break into established industries. However, the rise of the internet and social media has democratized content creation, enabling individuals to share their work directly with audiences without the need for intermediaries. This shift has paved the way for platforms like OnlyFans, which empower creators to monetize their content on their own terms.

As the online environment has matured, so too have the strategies and techniques employed by content creators. Models and influencers on platforms like OnlyFans have developed unique content creation strategies that cater to their specific audiences, leveraging both creativity and market research. Understanding the preferences and desires of subscribers is crucial, as successful creators continually adapt their offerings to maintain engagement. This evolution has also seen the emergence of niche markets, where individuals can carve out specific identities and connect with like-minded communities, further enhancing their potential for monetization.

Marketing techniques for OnlyFans creators have also transformed alongside technological advancements. Social media platforms serve as powerful tools for promotion, enabling creators to reach broader audiences and foster deeper connections with their fanbase. Effective marketing is not just about advertising; it involves storytelling and building a brand that resonates with potential subscribers. Creators must be adept at utilizing various social media channels to showcase their personalities and content, ensuring they maintain a consistent and authentic presence that attracts and retains subscribers.

In addition to subscriptions, many OnlyFans models have begun exploring alternative monetization methods to diversify their income streams. These methods can include selling exclusive merchandise, offering personalized content, or providing one-on-one interactions with fans. Such strategies not only enhance revenue potential but also foster a sense of community and loyalty among subscribers. By understanding the various ways to monetize their offerings, creators can build sustainable businesses that thrive in a competitive landscape.

Legal considerations play a vital role in the evolution of content creation, particularly for individuals operating in sensitive or stigmatized niches. Creators must be aware of copyright laws, privacy issues, and platform-specific regulations to protect their work and personal identity. Moreover, as the OnlyFans platform continues to evolve, staying informed about changes in policies and industry standards is imperative. By navigating these legal landscapes effectively, models can safeguard their businesses and cultivate an environment where creativity and entrepreneurship can flourish.

Running an OnlyFans Business

Setting Up Your Account

Setting up your OnlyFans account is the crucial first step in establishing your presence on the platform. Begin by visiting the OnlyFans website and clicking on the "Sign Up" button. You will need to provide a valid email address, create a strong password, and choose a username that reflects your brand identity. Choose a name that is memorable and aligns with the type of content you plan to create. Take your time to think about how you want to present yourself, as this will form the foundation of your brand on OnlyFans.

Once you have registered, you will need to verify your account. This process typically involves confirming your email address and providing some personal information. OnlyFans requires you to verify your identity by submitting a government-issued ID and a selfie for additional security. This step is essential not only for compliance with legal requirements but also for establishing trust with your audience. Ensuring your account is verified can enhance your credibility and help in building a loyal subscriber base.

After verification, you'll want to customize your profile to attract potential subscribers. This includes writing a compelling bio that highlights your unique personality and the type of content you will offer. Use engaging language that resonates with your target audience and clearly outlines what they can expect from your subscription. Additionally, set a subscription price that reflects the value of your content while remaining competitive within your niche. Offering introductory pricing or promotional discounts can also encourage initial sign-ups and help you gain traction.

The next step involves setting up your payment options. OnlyFans allows you to receive payments through various methods, including bank transfers and e-wallets. Make sure to choose a payment method that best suits your needs and is accessible to your audience. It's important to familiarize yourself with the platform's payout schedule and the fees associated with each payment option. Understanding these financial logistics will enable you to manage your earnings effectively and strategize for future growth.

Finally, consider how you will promote your OnlyFans account once it's set up. Utilize social media platforms to create awareness and direct traffic to your profile. Craft a marketing plan that includes regular updates, teasers of your content, and interactive engagement with your followers. Building an engaged community is key to sustaining your business, so leverage social media integration to connect with your audience on multiple levels. As you establish your presence, consistently evaluate your strategies and adapt them to enhance your visibility and subscriber growth.

Defining Your Niche

Defining your niche is a critical step in establishing a successful OnlyFans business. A well-defined niche allows you to differentiate yourself from the vast array of content creators on the platform. It helps you identify your target audience and tailor your content to meet their specific interests and desires. By narrowing your focus, you can create a more engaging and cohesive brand that resonates with subscribers. This clarity will not only guide your content creation strategies but also influence your marketing techniques, ensuring that your efforts are directed toward the right audience.

To effectively define your niche, start by assessing your interests, skills, and experiences. Consider what you are passionate about and how that can translate into content that others will find valuable or entertaining. Your background, personality, and unique attributes can serve as the foundation for your niche. For instance, if you have a background in fitness, you might consider creating content around workout routines, healthy living, or body positivity. By aligning your niche with your authentic self, you'll find it easier to engage with your subscribers and maintain motivation over the long term.

Understanding your target audience is equally important when defining your niche. Conduct research to identify the demographics, preferences, and behaviors of potential subscribers. This insight will help you tailor your content and marketing strategies effectively. Engaging with your audience through surveys or social media can provide valuable feedback and guidance. Additionally, exploring successful creators within your niche can offer inspiration and highlight the types of content that resonate well with subscribers, allowing you to refine your own approach.

Once you have a clearer understanding of your niche and audience, it's time to develop a strong brand identity. Your branding should reflect your niche while also showcasing your personality and values. This includes creating a compelling profile, choosing a consistent aesthetic, and developing a unique voice in your content. A well-defined brand not only attracts subscribers but also fosters loyalty, encouraging them to engage with your content and participate in your community. Remember that your brand extends beyond your On-lyFans page; it should be consistent across all platforms where you promote your content.

Finally, it's essential to remain adaptable as you grow and evolve within your niche. The landscape of content creation is dynamic, and your audience's preferences may shift over time. Regularly reassessing your niche and being open to experimentation can lead to new opportunities for growth and monetization. By staying attuned to industry trends and subscriber feedback, you can refine your content strategies and explore monetization methods beyond subscriptions, such as merchandise, exclusive content, or personalized experiences, ensuring the sustainability and success of your OnlyFans business.

Creating a Business Plan

Creating a business plan is a crucial step for OnlyFans models and creators aiming to maximize their success on the platform. A well-structured business plan serves not only as a roadmap for your content creation and monetization strategies but also as a tool to clarify your goals, identify your target audience, and outline your marketing techniques. Begin by defining your brand identity—what sets you apart from others on OnlyFans. Consider your niche, personal story, and the type of content you want to create, as these elements will help you resonate with your desired audience.

Next, analyze the competitive landscape. Research other creators within your niche to understand their offerings, pricing strategies, and audience engagement techniques. This analysis will inform your content creation strategies, allowing you to innovate and differentiate your offerings. Identify gaps in the market that you can fill and consider how your unique skills and experiences can enhance your content. This competitive insight will also aid in developing effective marketing techniques tailored to your audience's preferences.

Financial planning is another essential component of your business plan. Outline your projected income from subscriptions, tips, and any additional monetization methods such as merchandise or exclusive content. Factor in your expenses, which may include production costs, promotional efforts, and platform fees. Understanding these financial dynamics will not only help you set realistic goals but also enable you to manage your finances and taxes effectively. Ensuring that your financial projections are grounded in reality will provide a clearer picture of your potential earnings and sustainability.

Building an engaged community is vital for long-term success on OnlyFans. Your business plan should include strategies for fostering relationships with your subscribers and creating a loyal fan base. Consider the use of social media integration to promote your OnlyFans page and engage with your audience on multiple platforms. Regularly interacting with your followers, offering personalized content, and responding to their feedback will enhance their overall experience, encouraging them to remain subscribed and support your growth.

Finally, it is important to address legal considerations within your business plan. Understand the terms of service for OnlyFans and familiarize yourself with copyright issues, tax obligations, and any local regulations that may impact your content creation. By proactively addressing these legal aspects, you will not only protect your work but also build a solid foundation for your business. A comprehensive business plan that encompasses all of these elements will empower you to navigate the challenges of creating and monetizing content on OnlyFans effectively.

Content Creation Strategies for OnlyFans

Types of Content to Create

When embarking on an OnlyFans journey, understanding the types of content you can create is crucial for attracting and retaining subscribers. Diverse content types not only keep your audience engaged but also provide opportunities for monetization beyond standard subscription fees. Visual content, such as photos and videos, is the backbone of the platform. High-quality images that showcase your personality and unique style can significantly contribute to your brand identity. Experimenting with different themes, outfits, and settings can help you discover what resonates best with your audience.

In addition to visual content, consider creating behind-the-scenes material that offers subscribers a glimpse into your daily life and the creative process. This type of content fosters a sense of intimacy and authenticity, which can deepen the connection with your audience. Sharing your journey, including your challenges and successes, can make subscribers feel more invested in your story. Engaging your audience in this way not only builds loyalty but can also encourage them to share your content with others, effectively expanding your reach.

Interactive content is another powerful tool for OnlyFans creators. Polls, Q&A sessions, and live streams provide opportunities for real-time engagement, allowing subscribers to feel more involved in your content. These interactions can also serve as a platform for feedback, helping you tailor future content to better meet the desires of your audience. Moreover, live sessions can create a sense of urgency and exclusivity, prompting subscribers to participate and engage immediately.

Educational content can set you apart from other creators and position you as an expert in your niche. Whether it's sharing tips on self-care, fitness routines, or even financial advice for managing income from OnlyFans, educational content can add value to your subscribers' lives. This not only enhances your credibility but can also attract a broader audience who may be interested in your expertise beyond just adult content.

Lastly, consider integrating themed content into your strategy. Seasonal events, holidays, or trending topics can provide fresh and relevant material that keeps your profile dynamic. By aligning your content with these themes, you can capitalize on existing interests and encourage subscribers to return for new experiences. Creating a content calendar that incorporates these diverse types can streamline your creation process and ensure that you consistently deliver engaging material that keeps your audience coming back for more.

Content Scheduling and Consistency

Content scheduling and consistency are pivotal for success on OnlyFans. Establishing a regular posting schedule helps to create anticipation among your subscribers, fostering a sense of reliability that can significantly enhance subscriber retention. When followers know when to expect new content, they are more likely to stay engaged and renew their subscriptions. This predictability not only aids in cultivating a loyal community but also encourages subscribers to engage more actively with your content, leading to higher interaction rates and potential upselling opportunities.

To optimize your content scheduling, consider using a content calendar. This tool allows you to plan and organize your posts in advance, ensuring a balanced mix of content types. You can incorporate various formats such as photos, videos, and live streams, while also aligning your schedule with relevant dates or events that resonate with your audience. For instance, special occasions or themed content can attract more subscribers and keep your current audience excited. Consistency in posting helps maintain your visibility on the platform, which is crucial for attracting new subscribers.

In addition to scheduling, maintaining a consistent brand identity across your content is essential. Your personal branding should reflect your unique style and the themes of your content. Whether you are focusing on fitness, lifestyle, or adult entertainment, ensuring that your visual and thematic elements align will create a cohesive experience for your audience. This consistency builds trust and recognition, making it easier for potential subscribers to identify with your brand and feel more inclined to support you financially.

Engagement is another key aspect of consistency. Regular interaction with your audience fosters a sense of community that can enhance subscriber loyalty. Responding to comments, hosting Q&A sessions, and asking for feedback on your content not only builds rapport but also helps you understand what your audience values. This two-way communication can guide your future content creation, ensuring that you meet the evolving interests of your subscribers while maintaining a steady flow of engaging material.

Finally, it is important to be adaptable within your scheduling and content strategy. While consistency is crucial, being flexible allows you to respond to trends and audience feedback effectively. Monitor your analytics to understand which types of content perform best and adjust your schedule accordingly. This balance between consistency and adaptability will help you maintain a thriving OnlyFans business that can withstand the changing dynamics of the platform and its audience.

Engaging with Subscribers through Content

Engaging with subscribers through content is a pivotal aspect of running a successful OnlyFans business. The relationship you build with your subscribers can significantly influence retention rates and overall profitability. To foster engagement, it is essential to understand your audience's preferences, desires, and pain points. Engage them by asking for feedback, conducting polls, or simply encouraging them to share their thoughts about your content. This open channel of communication not only builds rapport but also allows you to tailor your offerings to better meet their needs.

Content variety plays a crucial role in keeping subscribers interested. Experiment with different formats such as photos, videos, live streams, and even exclusive behind-the-scenes content. The diversity in content types can captivate a broader audience and maintain the interest of long-term subscribers. Regularly updating your content and introducing themed series or special events can also create excitement and anticipation among your subscribers, making them more likely to stay engaged and renew their subscriptions.

Interactivity is another powerful tool for enhancing subscriber engagement. Consider hosting Q&A sessions or live chats where subscribers can interact with you in real time. This not only personalizes the experience but also makes subscribers feel valued and included. Additionally, offering personalized content such as custom videos or shout-outs can create a deeper connection, encouraging subscribers to invest more in your brand. The more interactive your content, the more likely subscribers are to feel a sense of belonging within your community.

Building a community around your OnlyFans brand can further enhance subscriber engagement. Utilize social media platforms to create discussions and share highlights from your OnlyFans content. Encourage subscribers to share their experiences and connect with each other, fostering a sense of belonging. Creating a dedicated space, such as a Discord server or a private Facebook group, can also facilitate ongoing conversations and strengthen the community. When subscribers feel like they are part of something larger, they are more likely to remain loyal and engaged.

Finally, maintaining a consistent brand identity across all your content is crucial. Your brand should reflect your personality and resonate with your target audience. This consistency not only helps in establishing recognition but also builds trust. Ensure that your visuals, messaging, and overall tone align with your brand identity. By doing so, you will create a cohesive experience for your subscribers, making them feel more connected to you and your content. Engaging with subscribers through strategic content creation not only enhances their experience but also lays the foundation for a sustainable and profitable Only-Fans business.

4

Marketing Techniques for OnlyFans Creators

Social Media Marketing

Social media marketing is an essential tool for OnlyFans creators looking to expand their reach and maximize their income potential. Platforms like Instagram, Twitter, TikTok, and Snapchat provide unique opportunities to connect with audiences, showcase content, and drive traffic to your OnlyFans page. It is crucial to understand the distinct characteristics of each platform and tailor your approach accordingly. For instance, Instagram is highly visual and ideal for sharing enticing snapshots and behind-the-scenes content, while Twitter allows for more direct interaction and real-time engagement with followers.

To effectively leverage social media, creators should focus on building a strong personal brand that resonates with their target audience. This involves developing a consistent aesthetic across platforms, crafting a compelling bio, and using hashtags strategically to enhance discoverability. Engaging content should not only highlight your offerings on OnlyFans but also reflect your personality and interests, fostering a genuine connection with potential subscribers. By sharing relatable stories, insights, and exclusive previews, you can create a narrative that encourages followers to transition to your OnlyFans account.

Engagement is a two-way street in social media marketing. Responding to comments, participating in conversations, and recognizing loyal followers can significantly boost your online presence. Additionally, consider collaborating with other creators or influencers to tap into their audiences and expand your reach. Joint promotions, shout-outs, or guest appearances can introduce your content to new potential subscribers who might not have discovered you otherwise. Building a community around your brand will not only enhance your visibility but also create a loyal subscriber base.

Utilizing analytics tools available on social media platforms can provide valuable insights into your audience's behavior and preferences. Monitoring metrics such as engagement rates, follower growth, and content performance allows you to refine your strategy continuously. Understanding which posts resonate most with your audience can inform your content creation process, ensuring that you deliver what your followers want to see. This data-driven approach can lead to more effective marketing campaigns and higher conversion rates for your OnlyFans account.

Lastly, it's essential to navigate the legal considerations of social media marketing, particularly in the context of adult content. Familiarize yourself with the community guidelines of each platform to avoid potential bans or restrictions. Additionally, be mindful of privacy and safety concerns when sharing personal information or engaging with followers. Establishing clear boundaries and maintaining professionalism in your interactions will not only protect your brand but also foster a respectful and engaged community that supports your OnlyFans journey.

Influencer Collaborations

Influencer collaborations can significantly enhance your visibility and credibility as an OnlyFans creator. By partnering with established influencers in your niche, you tap into their audience and create opportunities for cross-promotion. This strategy not only broadens your reach but also allows you to leverage the influencer's established trust with their followers. Choose collaborators whose brand aligns with yours and whose audience shares interests that would likely resonate with your content. This alignment ensures that your collaboration feels authentic and will engage both your audiences effectively.

When planning a collaboration, consider the type of content you want to create together. Joint photo shoots, live streams, or exclusive content giveaways can create excitement and anticipation. It's essential to establish clear expectations and goals for the collaboration upfront. Decide on the content format, posting schedule, and how you will promote it across your respective platforms. Effective communication throughout the process is crucial to ensure that both parties feel valued and that the collaboration is a success.

Promotional strategies should be a pivotal part of your collaboration plan. Utilize both your and your collaborator's social media channels to tease the upcoming content. Behind-the-scenes footage or sneak peeks can build hype and engage your audiences ahead of the launch. Additionally, consider hosting a live Q&A session or an interactive event to deepen the connection with your followers. By actively involving your audiences in the collaboration, you increase the likelihood of them supporting both creators, which can lead to higher conversion rates on your OnlyFans page.

Measuring the success of influencer collaborations is vital to understanding their impact on your OnlyFans business. Track metrics such as new subscribers, engagement rates, and overall content performance to assess the effectiveness of your joint efforts. This analysis will help you identify what worked well and what could be improved for future collaborations. Being data-driven allows you to refine your strategies, ensuring that each partnership contributes positively to your growth and monetization objectives.

Finally, be mindful of the legal considerations surrounding influencer collaborations. Ensure that both parties have a clear agreement regarding content ownership, usage rights, and revenue sharing. This transparency not only protects you legally but also fosters a professional relationship built on trust. By approaching collaborations with a strategic mindset and an understanding of the legal implications, you can create mutually beneficial partnerships that elevate your OnlyFans brand and enhance your overall content creation efforts.

Email Marketing Strategies

Email marketing is a powerful tool for OnlyFans models looking to enhance their reach and drive engagement with their audience. Unlike social media platforms, where algorithms dictate visibility, email allows creators to maintain direct communication with their subscribers. By building an email list, you can share exclusive content, special offers, and personal updates directly to your fans, ensuring they feel valued and connected to your brand. It is essential to create a strategy that focuses on capturing emails effectively and nurturing these contacts over time.

To start, consider offering an incentive for your audience to subscribe to your email list. This could be a free exclusive photo set, a discount on subscriptions, or access to intimate live chats. Once you have captured these leads, ensure that your emails are valuable and engaging. Craft messages that reflect your personality and brand, and segment your audience based on their preferences or interaction levels. This personalization can significantly increase engagement rates, turning casual fans into loyal supporters.

Regularly scheduled newsletters can be an excellent way to keep your audience informed and engaged. Use these newsletters to share updates about your content, upcoming events, or collaborations. Highlighting user-generated content or fan testimonials can also foster community spirit and encourage more interaction. Additionally, consider including links to your social media platforms to drive cross-channel engagement, allowing your fans to connect with you in various spaces.

Pay attention to analytics to understand what types of content resonate best with your audience. Track open rates, click-through rates, and subscriber growth to refine your strategy continually. A/B testing different subject lines or content formats can provide valuable insights into your audience's preferences. Utilizing these metrics will help you streamline your email marketing efforts and ensure that your messages remain relevant and enticing.

Finally, be mindful of the legal considerations surrounding email marketing. Familiarize yourself with regulations such as the CAN-SPAM Act, which governs how you can communicate with your subscribers. Provide clear opt-in options, and always include an easy way for subscribers to opt-out of your list. Building trust with your audience is paramount, and transparency about how you handle their information will contribute to a positive and lasting relationship, ultimately enhancing your OnlyFans business.

5

Monetization Methods Beyond Subscriptions

Pay-Per-View Content

Pay-Per-View (PPV) content is a powerful monetization strategy that allows OnlyFans creators to maximize their earnings beyond the traditional subscription model. By offering exclusive content that users must pay to access, creators can cater to specific interests and desires, providing a tailored experience that encourages fans to invest more in their favorite creators. This method not only increases revenue but also enhances the perceived value of the content being shared, creating a win-win scenario for both creators and subscribers.

To effectively implement PPV content, it is essential to identify the types of content that resonate with your audience. This could range from personalized messages, custom photos, or videos to exclusive behind-the-scenes access. Understanding your niche and what your audience craves will enable you to create compelling offers that entice subscribers to pay for one-time access. Additionally, promoting upcoming PPV content through your regular posts can create anticipation and drive sales, allowing you to leverage your existing subscriber base effectively.

Marketing your PPV content requires strategic communication and engagement with your audience. Utilize your social media platforms to tease upcoming content and generate buzz. Engaging with your followers through polls or questions can help gauge their interest in specific types of PPV content, ensuring that what you create aligns with their desires. Furthermore, consider offering limited-time deals or bundles to incentivize purchases, enhancing the urgency and appeal of your offers.

Legal considerations should also be at the forefront of your mind when creating and selling PPV content. Ensure that all content adheres to platform guidelines and local laws regarding adult content. It's crucial to protect your intellectual property while also being aware of any regulations surrounding the sale of explicit materials. Consulting with a legal professional experienced in digital content can provide clarity and safeguard your business against potential pitfalls.

Lastly, building an engaged community around your PPV offerings is essential for long-term success. Encourage feedback and interaction from your subscribers to foster a sense of belonging and loyalty. By making your fans feel valued and heard, they are more likely to invest in your PPV content and promote your brand to others. Building relationships through personalized interactions can enhance the overall experience for your subscribers, ultimately leading to increased sales and a more sustainable income stream.

Tips and Donations

Incorporating tips and donations into your OnlyFans strategy can significantly enhance your income and foster a deeper connection with your audience. Many subscribers are willing to go the extra mile to show appreciation for the content you produce. To effectively encourage tipping, ensure your content is not only high-quality but also interactive. Consider hosting live streams, Q&A sessions, or personalized shout-outs where fans can tip in real-time as a way to engage with you. The more personal and interactive your content, the more likely subscribers will feel compelled to tip.

Another effective strategy is to create exclusive content that is unlocked through tips. For example, you might offer a special video or photo set that is only accessible after a subscriber tips a certain amount. This approach creates a sense of urgency and exclusivity, motivating fans to contribute financially. Clearly communicate these opportunities through your posts and messages, ensuring subscribers understand how tipping directly supports your content creation efforts.

Highlighting the benefits they receive in return can drive more users to contribute.

Additionally, consider utilizing donation platforms integrated into your OnlyFans account. Platforms like Ko-fi or Buy Me a Coffee allow fans to donate outside of the subscription model. Promote these options alongside your OnlyFans content, emphasizing that donations go directly toward enhancing your content quality, such as improved equipment or creative concepts. Transparency about how funds are utilized can build trust and encourage ongoing support from your community.

Engagement is crucial when it comes to tips and donations. Show gratitude to your supporters by acknowledging their contributions in your posts and messages. This could be as simple as a thank-you shout-out or featuring top tippers in a special segment. By recognizing your fans, you create a sense of community and belonging, which can lead to increased loyalty and repeat donations. The more valued your subscribers feel, the more likely they are to continue supporting you financially.

Lastly, promote a culture of tipping by sharing success stories and testimonials from other creators who have benefited from this approach. Highlighting the financial freedom and creative opportunities that can arise from receiving tips can inspire your audience to engage in similar practices. By establishing an environment where tipping is normalized and appreciated, you can cultivate a more robust income stream that complements your subscription model and enhances your overall OnlyFans business.

Selling Merchandise

Selling merchandise can be a powerful avenue for OnlyFans creators to diversify their income and enhance their brand identity. Beyond subscriptions, merchandise offers a tangible connection between creators and their audience, allowing fans to engage with you in a more personal way. From branded apparel to exclusive digital products, the potential for revenue generation is vast, but it requires a strategic approach to design, marketing, and fulfillment. Understanding your audience's preferences and aligning your merchandise with your brand can create a loyal fanbase willing to invest in your creative output.

To successfully launch merchandise, it is essential to conduct thorough market research. Analyze what types of products resonate with your current subscribers and consider their feedback. Engaging with your audience through polls or direct messages can provide insights into their preferences. For instance, if you have a gaming-focused Only-Fans account, merchandise like branded gaming gear or themed clothing might be particularly appealing. Tailoring your offerings to fit your niche not only increases the likelihood of sales but also strengthens your brand's identity.

Once you have identified potential products, designing your merchandise is the next critical step. Ensure that your designs reflect your personal brand and resonate with your audience. Collaborating with graphic designers can elevate the quality of your merchandise, making it more appealing. Additionally, consider incorporating limited edition items or exclusive merchandise to create urgency and encourage immediate purchases.

Highlighting the uniqueness of your products can entice fans to buy them, knowing they are part of a select group.

Marketing your merchandise effectively involves integrating your promotional efforts with your overall content strategy. Utilize your Only-Fans platform to showcase your products through engaging content, such as behind-the-scenes videos or photoshoots featuring the merchandise. Social media channels can also amplify your reach; share eye-catching visuals and stories that resonate with your audience. Collaborating with influencers or other creators can further expand your audience and generate buzz around your merchandise launches, creating a community-driven approach to promotion.

Finally, managing the logistics of selling merchandise is crucial for a seamless experience. Choose a reliable platform for production and fulfillment, ensuring that quality and delivery times meet your audience's expectations. Establish clear pricing strategies that account for production costs while remaining competitive. Additionally, consider the legal and financial implications of your merchandise sales, such as taxation and copyright issues. Staying informed about these aspects will not only protect your brand but also enhance your professionalism in the marketplace. By addressing these key areas, you can successfully integrate merchandise sales into your OnlyFans business model, ultimately increasing your revenue and solidifying your brand presence.

6

Building an Engaged Community on OnlyFans

The Importance of Engagement

Engagement is a cornerstone of success for OnlyFans creators, significantly influencing both subscriber retention and overall revenue. In an increasingly competitive landscape, where numerous models vie for attention, establishing a strong connection with your audience becomes essential. Engagement is not merely about attracting subscribers; it's about fostering a community that feels valued and connected to you. When subscribers see themselves as part of your journey, they are more likely to remain loyal and invest in additional content or services you offer.

Creating quality content is crucial, but without engagement, even the best content can fall flat. Engagement goes beyond posting photos or videos; it involves interaction, responsiveness, and a genuine interest in your audience's preferences. Techniques such as polls, Q&A sessions, and direct messages can cultivate a sense of involvement. By actively seeking feedback and encouraging dialogue, you empower your subscribers to feel like co-creators of your content. This not only enhances their experience but also drives them to spread the word about your page, leading to organic growth.

Marketing plays a vital role in driving subscribers to your OnlyFans account, but engagement will keep them coming back. Building a personal brand that resonates with your audience fosters a sense of loyalty. Sharing behind-the-scenes content and personal stories can humanize your brand and create an emotional connection. When subscribers feel they know you personally, they are less likely to cancel their subscriptions. Moreover, loyal fans are more inclined to support you through tips, special requests, or purchases of exclusive content, enhancing your monetization potential.

Legal considerations should not overshadow the importance of engagement. Navigating the complexities of content creation and adult work requires a solid understanding of legality and ethics. Engaging with your audience helps establish trust, which is crucial in this domain. When your subscribers feel secure in their interactions with you and your content, they are more inclined to remain engaged and supportive, reducing the likelihood of disputes or misunderstandings.

In summary, engagement is not just a supplementary aspect of running an OnlyFans business; it is fundamental to your success. By fostering a vibrant community, creating personal connections, and ensuring transparent communication, you not only enhance the subscriber experience but also improve your revenue potential. As you navigate the challenges of content creation and monetization, remember that a well-engaged audience is your greatest asset, capable of propelling your OnlyFans venture to new heights.

Strategies for Community Building

Building a successful community around your OnlyFans presence is crucial for long-term success and engagement. A strong community fosters loyalty among subscribers, encourages repeat business, and can enhance your overall brand image. The first strategy for effective community building is to engage authentically with your audience. This involves responding to messages and comments, asking for feedback, and showing appreciation for your subscribers. By creating an environment where your fans feel heard and valued, you can cultivate a sense of belonging that encourages them to remain active members of your community.

Another vital aspect of community building is the creation of exclusive content that resonates with your audience's interests. Consider what your subscribers enjoy most and tailor content to meet those preferences. This could be through polls, Q&A sessions, or themed content days. By involving your audience in the content creation process, you not only keep them engaged but also empower them to feel like they are part of your creative journey. Regularly refreshing your content and providing unique experiences will keep subscribers excited and invested in your platform.

Utilizing social media effectively can significantly enhance your community-building efforts. Platforms like Twitter, Instagram, and TikTok can serve as extensions of your OnlyFans brand, allowing you to connect with potential subscribers. Share behind-the-scenes content, personal stories, and sneak peeks of upcoming posts to build anticipation. Creating a cohesive brand presence across these platforms helps to establish your identity and attract followers who are likely to convert into subscribers. Additionally, collaborating with other creators can introduce you to new audiences and expand your network.

Hosting events or special promotions can further strengthen community ties. Consider organizing live streams, virtual meet-and-greets, or subscriber-only contests that incentivize participation and interaction. These events not only provide entertainment but also create memorable experiences that reinforce subscriber loyalty. Such initiatives can lead to organic growth as satisfied subscribers promote your content to their networks, expanding your reach and visibility.

Finally, establishing clear guidelines and maintaining a positive atmosphere within your community is essential. This includes setting boundaries regarding acceptable behavior and moderation practices. A respectful and safe environment encourages participation and fosters inclusivity, which is crucial for diverse audiences. By prioritizing community health and addressing issues promptly, you ensure that your space remains welcoming, allowing your brand to flourish on OnlyFans.

Hosting Events and Live Streams

Hosting events and live streams can significantly enhance your OnlyFans presence, providing a unique and engaging experience for your subscribers. These live interactions allow you to connect with your audience in real-time, creating a sense of intimacy and exclusivity that is often missing from pre-recorded content. By planning events such as Q&A sessions, themed parties, or even casual chats, you can foster a deeper connection with your fans, encouraging loyalty and increasing retention rates. The key is to promote these events effectively across your social media platforms, ensuring your audience is aware of the upcoming opportunities to engage with you directly.

When it comes to choosing the type of event to host, consider what resonates most with your audience. Poll your subscribers to gauge their interests, whether it be interactive games, tutorials, or behind-the-scenes glimpses into your life or content creation process. Tailoring your events to meet the desires of your audience not only increases participation but also enhances their overall satisfaction with your content. Additionally, special events like birthday celebrations, holiday themes, or collaborations with other content creators can draw in new subscribers while keeping your current audience excited and engaged.

Live streaming offers a dynamic way to monetize your content beyond traditional subscriptions.

By incorporating ticketed events or exclusive access to certain live sessions, you can create additional revenue streams. Consider offering VIP experiences where fans can pay for one-on-one interactions or personalized shoutouts during the stream. This approach not only boosts your income but also reinforces the notion of exclusivity, making your subscribers feel valued and appreciated. Make sure to clearly communicate the benefits of attending these events and what they can expect in return for their investment.

To maximize the success of your live streams and events, invest in quality equipment and a reliable internet connection. Clear audio and video are essential for keeping your audience engaged and ensuring a professional presentation. Additionally, familiarize yourself with the platform's features, such as chat moderation and interactive tools, to enhance the viewer experience. Engaging with your audience during the stream by responding to comments and questions in real-time can create a lively atmosphere, making attendees feel more connected and involved.

Finally, after your event, take the time to solicit feedback from your audience. Understanding what they enjoyed and what could be improved will help you refine future events and live streams. Consider creating highlight reels or recap content that you can share on your OnlyFans page and social media, allowing those who missed the event to engage with the content later. By consistently hosting compelling events and live streams, you not only boost your visibility and subscriber count but also solidify your brand as an interactive and engaging creator within the OnlyFans community.

Legal Considerations for OnlyFans Creators

Understanding Copyright and Ownership

Understanding copyright and ownership is crucial for anyone in the realm of content creation, particularly for OnlyFans models and creators. Copyright law grants creators exclusive rights over their original works, allowing them to control how their content is used, shared, and monetized. This legal framework protects creators from unauthorized use and exploitation of their content, ensuring that they can capitalize on their creativity. As you embark on your journey in content creation, it is essential to familiarize yourself with the nuances of copyright to safeguard your intellectual property effectively.

Ownership of content is another vital aspect that OnlyFans creators must grasp. When you produce original content, such as photos, videos, or written material, you automatically hold the copyright to that work as the creator. However, many creators unknowingly grant additional rights to platforms like OnlyFans through their terms of service. Understanding these agreements is essential, as they can impact how you retain ownership of your content and how it may be used by the platform or others. Clear awareness of these terms allows you to navigate potential pitfalls and maintain control over your brand and creations.

In addition to understanding copyright, it is important to recognize the implications of sharing your content online. Once content is published, it can be difficult to control its dissemination. Unauthorized sharing or reposting can occur, which may dilute your brand and affect your potential earnings. To mitigate these risks, consider watermarking your images or using delayed posting strategies. By taking proactive steps to protect your work, you can maintain your exclusivity and ensure that your audience appreciates the value of your content.

Legal considerations extend beyond copyright ownership, encompassing issues related to consent, privacy, and modeling agreements. As an OnlyFans creator, you may collaborate with other individuals or hire professionals for photography and videography. It is vital to have clear agreements in place that outline ownership and usage rights for any collaborative work. This not only protects your interests but also fosters a professional relationship with collaborators, ensuring that all parties understand their rights and obligations regarding the content produced.

Finally, maintaining a strong personal brand is intertwined with understanding copyright and ownership. Your brand is a reflection of your identity and the unique content you offer. By safeguarding your intellectual property, you reinforce your brand's integrity and value in the eyes of your audience. This, in turn, can lead to increased engagement and loyalty from your subscribers. As you create and monetize your content on Only-Fans, prioritize your copyright and ownership to build a sustainable and successful online presence.

Privacy and Consent Issues

Privacy and consent are paramount concerns for OnlyFans creators, as the nature of the platform requires sharing personal content with subscribers. Models must carefully navigate the fine line between building a relatable personal brand and safeguarding their privacy. One essential strategy is to establish clear boundaries regarding what content is shared, ensuring that only material that aligns with personal comfort levels is made public. This not only protects personal privacy but also helps to cultivate a more authentic connection with followers, fostering trust and engagement.

Consent is another critical aspect of content creation on OnlyFans. It is vital that creators understand the legal implications surrounding the sharing of explicit content. This includes obtaining explicit consent from any individuals featured in the content, whether they are collaborators or simply appear in the background. Additionally, creators should familiarize themselves with the platform's policies regarding content usage and distribution to prevent potential legal issues. Building a strong understanding of consent not only protects creators legally but also enhances their professional reputation within the adult content industry.

To further mitigate privacy risks, models should consider utilizing pseudonyms and anonymizing personal information linked to their OnlyFans accounts. By separating their personal lives from their online personas, creators can maintain a level of anonymity that is often necessary in adult content work. This can also extend to the use of secure payment methods and keeping personal contact information private. Such measures not only protect against unwanted attention but also enhance the overall safety and security of the creator's personal life.

Engaging with subscribers while maintaining privacy is a delicate balance. Creators can foster a sense of community through interactive content, such as live streams or Q&A sessions, while being mindful not to divulge personal details that could compromise their safety. Using features like private messaging can allow for more intimate interactions without sacrificing anonymity. It's essential for models to set clear guidelines on what types of interactions are acceptable, ensuring that both they and their subscribers feel comfortable and respected.

Ultimately, prioritizing privacy and consent is crucial for the long-term success of an OnlyFans business. By establishing and communicating clear boundaries, understanding legal frameworks, and employing strategies that protect personal identity, creators can build a sustainable and rewarding presence on the platform. This not only enhances the creator's experience but also sets a standard for professionalism within the industry, encouraging a culture of respect and responsibility among all participants.

Navigating Adult Content Regulations

Navigating the landscape of adult content regulations is crucial for OnlyFans creators aiming to maintain compliance while maximizing their earning potential. Adult content is subject to a variety of laws and regulations that may differ significantly between jurisdictions. Understanding these legal frameworks is essential for models and content creators who wish to operate within the boundaries of the law. It is advisable to familiarize oneself with both local and international regulations regarding adult content, as failure to comply can result in severe penalties, including fines and the potential shutdown of accounts.

One of the primary legal considerations for OnlyFans creators is age verification. Models must ensure that all participants in their content are at least 18 years old and can provide valid identification. Platforms like OnlyFans have implemented strict age verification processes to protect both creators and subscribers. It is crucial to keep thorough records of age verification to safeguard against potential legal issues. Additionally, understanding the implications of content involving nudity, sexual acts, or explicit material can help creators navigate potential restrictions imposed by payment processors and financial institutions.

Content creators must also be aware of the regulations surrounding the distribution and sharing of adult content. Many regions have specific laws regarding the sharing of explicit material, particularly when it comes to consent and copyright. Models should always obtain explicit consent from anyone featured in their content and be diligent about protecting their intellectual property. This includes watermarking images and videos, as well as being cautious about sharing content on other platforms. Understanding how to legally protect one's content can help prevent unauthorized distribution and exploitation.

Marketing strategies for adult content must also take into account the restrictions imposed by various social media platforms. Many mainstream platforms have stringent policies against adult content, which can complicate promotional efforts. Creators must navigate these policies carefully, utilizing alternative marketing techniques, such as building a dedicated website or using niche social media platforms that are more accepting of adult content. By developing a strong brand identity and community engagement strategy, models can effectively promote their OnlyFans accounts while staying within legal boundaries.

Finally, it is imperative for OnlyFans creators to maintain transparency with their subscribers regarding the nature of their content and any potential risks associated with adult material. Clear communication helps build trust and fosters a supportive community. Moreover, creators should remain informed about any changes in laws or regulations that could impact their business. By prioritizing compliance and legal understanding, OnlyFans models can create a sustainable and profitable venture while minimizing risks associated with adult content creation.

8

Branding and Personal Identity for OnlyFans

Developing Your Brand Identity

Developing a strong brand identity is essential for OnlyFans creators who want to stand out in a competitive landscape. Your brand identity encompasses your unique style, messaging, and the overall experience you provide to your subscribers. It begins with understanding who you are as a creator, what you wish to convey through your content, and how you want your audience to perceive you. Take the time to define your values, mission, and vision. This foundational work will inform every aspect of your brand and guide your decisions as you create content and engage with your audience.

Once you have a clear understanding of your identity, the next step is to create a visual representation of your brand. This includes elements such as your logo, color palette, and typography. Consistency in visuals helps reinforce your brand and makes it easily recognizable. Invest in high-quality graphics and consider how your visual identity will translate across various platforms, including your OnlyFans page and social media channels. Remember that your visuals should reflect the tone and personality of your content, whether that's playful, edgy, luxurious, or professional.

Your brand messaging is equally important, as it shapes the way you communicate with your audience. Develop a distinctive voice that reflects your personality and resonates with your target audience. This includes the language you use, the themes you explore in your content, and the way you interact with your subscribers. Authenticity is crucial; your followers are more likely to engage with content that feels genuine and relatable. Use storytelling to connect with your audience on a deeper level, sharing your journey, experiences, and aspirations to foster a sense of community.

Building an engaged community is a vital part of your brand identity. Engage with your subscribers through regular communication and interaction, such as responding to comments, hosting Q&A sessions, or creating polls. Encourage feedback and make your audience feel valued by incorporating their suggestions into your content. This engagement not only strengthens your relationship with your current subscribers but also helps attract new ones, as potential followers are drawn to creators who actively involve their audience in their journey.

Finally, consider the legal aspects of your brand identity. Ensure that your content adheres to OnlyFans guidelines and local laws, particularly regarding adult content. Protect your brand by understanding copyright laws and securing the necessary permissions for any third-party materials you use. This not only safeguards your work but also enhances your professional image. By developing a solid brand identity that encompasses your values, visuals, messaging, community engagement, and legal considerations, you will position yourself for long-term success on OnlyFans and beyond.

Crafting Your Personal Narrative

Crafting your personal narrative is a crucial step in establishing a successful OnlyFans presence. Your narrative is more than just your story; it is the foundation upon which your brand is built. It communicates who you are, what you offer, and why potential subscribers should choose you over others. To begin shaping your narrative, consider your unique experiences, values, and the message you wish to convey. This is not just about your background; it's about how your journey informs your content and connects with your audience.

A compelling personal narrative resonates with authenticity. Audiences are drawn to creators who are genuine and relatable. Share your motivations for joining OnlyFans and what you hope to achieve. This transparency can create a sense of intimacy, fostering a stronger connection with your subscribers. Your narrative should reflect your personality and highlight the aspects of your life that make you unique, whether that's your interests, your artistic vision, or your goals. Emphasizing these elements can enhance your appeal and encourage engagement.

In addition to authenticity, your narrative should also address your target audience's desires and needs. Understand who your subscribers are and what they seek in a creator. Tailoring your story to resonate with their interests can significantly impact your ability to build an engaged community. Consider how your experiences and insights can provide value to your audience. This could mean offering advice, sharing personal stories, or creating content that reflects their aspirations. The more you align your narrative with your audience's expectations, the more likely they are to invest in your content.

Visual storytelling plays a vital role in conveying your personal narrative. Use photography and videography not just to showcase your physical appearance, but to tell a story that underscores your brand. High-quality visuals can enhance your narrative, allowing subscribers to connect with you on a deeper level. Invest time in creating a consistent aesthetic that reflects your personality and values. Whether it's through themed photo shoots, behind-the-scenes videos, or personal vlogs, your visual content should complement and amplify your narrative.

Lastly, remember that your personal narrative is not static; it can evolve as you grow and change. Regularly revisiting and updating your story can keep your content fresh and engaging. As you gain experience and develop new interests, reflect these changes in your narrative. This adaptability not only keeps your audience engaged but also reinforces your brand's authenticity. By continuously crafting and refining your personal narrative, you can build a loyal subscriber base that feels connected to your journey and invested in your success.

Visual Branding Elements

Visual branding elements are crucial for establishing a memorable presence on OnlyFans, as they create an immediate connection with your audience. These elements include your logo, color scheme, typography, and overall aesthetic, which together form the visual identity of your brand. A coherent and appealing visual identity not only attracts potential subscribers but also fosters trust and loyalty among your existing audience. By consciously curating these elements, you can differentiate yourself in a crowded market and convey the values and personality of your brand.

The logo serves as the cornerstone of your visual branding. It is often the first thing that potential subscribers will notice, making it imperative that it encapsulates your brand's essence. A well-designed logo should be simple yet distinctive, allowing for easy recognition across various platforms. Consider the emotions and imagery you wish to evoke and ensure that your logo aligns with the type of content you create. Whether your brand leans towards playful, edgy, or sophisticated, your logo should clearly reflect that identity to attract the right audience.

Color schemes play a significant role in influencing perceptions and emotions. Different colors evoke different feelings, and choosing a palette that resonates with your target demographic can enhance your overall appeal. For instance, brighter colors may suggest energy and playfulness, while muted tones may convey elegance and sophistication. Consistency in your color scheme across all content will help reinforce your brand identity and make your posts instantly recognizable. This consistency not only aids in brand recall but also enhances the aesthetic quality of your content, making it more engaging for viewers.

Typography is another vital aspect of visual branding that is often overlooked. The fonts you choose should complement your overall design and align with the voice of your brand. Whether you opt for sleek, modern fonts or more whimsical, decorative typefaces, ensure that they are legible and reflect the personality you want to portray. Creating a hierarchy in your text through varying font sizes and styles can also guide viewers' attention to important information, such as promotional offers or key content highlights, making your messaging more effective.

Finally, the overall aesthetic of your content should harmonize with your visual branding elements. This includes the style of your photography and videography, the settings you choose, and the mood you create in your content. A cohesive aesthetic will not only draw in your audience but also keep them engaged, as they come to expect a certain quality and style from your posts. By meticulously crafting your visual branding elements, you can establish a strong, recognizable identity on OnlyFans that resonates with your audience and supports your business goals.

9

Photography and Videography Tips for OnlyFans

Equipment and Setup

When embarking on a journey as an OnlyFans creator, the right equipment and setup are crucial for producing high-quality content that resonates with your audience. A professional-grade camera is an essential investment, as it significantly impacts the visual appeal of your photos and videos. While many smartphones come equipped with impressive cameras, a dedicated DSLR or mirrorless camera can elevate your content further. Consider lenses that cater to your specific shooting style, whether that be portrait photography or wider shots for dynamic scenes. Additionally, a tripod will ensure stability, allowing for sharp images and smooth video recording, which is vital for creating polished content that stands out in a competitive market.

Lighting is another critical aspect of your setup. Natural light can be beneficial, but relying solely on it can lead to inconsistent results, especially if you are shooting at different times of the day. Investing in softbox lights or ring lights will provide you with a controlled lighting environment, enhancing the quality of your visuals regardless of external conditions. Proper lighting not only enhances features and colors but also sets the mood for your content, which can be particularly important in niches that emphasize aesthetics and atmosphere. Experimenting with different lighting setups will allow you to discover what works best for your brand and style.

Audio quality is often overlooked but is just as important as visual quality, especially for video content. Using an external microphone can markedly improve sound clarity, reducing background noise and capturing your voice in a more professional manner. This is particularly crucial if you plan to engage with your audience through videos or live streams, as poor audio can detract from the overall experience. Additionally, consider investing in soundproofing materials if you are recording in a space with significant echo or outside noise, ensuring that your audience receives the best possible audio experience.

Your setup should also include a dedicated workspace that reflects your brand identity. A clean, organized, and aesthetically pleasing background can enhance your content. Personalizing your space with props or decor that align with your niche will help convey your personality and create a memorable viewer experience. This is especially important in building a connection with your audience, as they are more likely to engage with creators who present a consistent and authentic image. Regularly updating your background and props can keep your content fresh and interesting, encouraging subscribers to remain engaged.

Lastly, consider the importance of digital tools in your content creation process. Software for editing photos and videos can elevate your final product, allowing for enhancements that improve overall quality. Familiarize yourself with programs such as Adobe Lightroom or Premiere Pro, which offer robust features for both photo and video editing. Additionally, tools for scheduling posts and managing social media can streamline your marketing efforts, freeing up time to focus on content creation. By integrating the right equipment, a well-thought-out setup, and effective digital tools, you will be better positioned to attract and retain subscribers while maximizing your revenue potential on OnlyFans.

Lighting Techniques

Lighting plays a crucial role in the quality of content created for OnlyFans, directly influencing how your audience perceives your images and videos. Proper lighting can enhance your features, create an inviting atmosphere, and convey the desired mood for your content. Understanding different lighting techniques can elevate your work, making it more professional and appealing to potential subscribers. Whether you are shooting at home or in a more controlled environment, the right lighting setup can help you achieve stunning visuals that stand out in a crowded marketplace.

Natural light is one of the most accessible and flattering lighting sources available. Utilizing daylight can create soft, even illumination that enhances skin tones and reduces harsh shadows. Positioning yourself near a window during the day can provide a beautiful, diffused light that is ideal for portrait shots. Experimenting with the time of day can yield different effects; early morning or late afternoon light, often referred to as the golden hour, can add warmth and depth to your images. However, relying solely on natural light can be unpredictable, so it's essential to have alternative options available, especially for evening shoots or in less-than-ideal weather conditions.

For those looking to invest in their content creation, artificial lighting offers greater control and consistency. Ring lights are popular among content creators for their ability to provide even, flattering light that minimizes shadows. These lights are particularly effective for close-up shots, such as selfies or beauty content. Softbox lights and LED panels are other options that can mimic natural light, providing a more professional look. When using artificial lighting, it is crucial to adjust the intensity and direction to create the desired effect, whether it's a dramatic look with shadows or a soft, glowing ambiance.

In addition to choosing the right light sources, understanding how to manipulate them can significantly enhance your content. Three-point lighting is a classic technique that involves using a key light, fill light, and backlight to create depth and dimension. The key light serves as the main source of illumination, while the fill light reduces shadows created by the key light, and the backlight adds separation from the background. Experimenting with different angles and distances can help you find the perfect balance, enhancing your overall aesthetic and making your content more visually appealing.

Finally, remember that post-production editing can further refine your lighting choices. Software tools allow you to adjust brightness, contrast, and color balance, helping to enhance the final product. However, it's important to strike a balance; over-editing can result in an unnatural look that may deter potential subscribers. Developing a signature style that aligns with your brand can create a cohesive visual identity across your OnlyFans profile. By mastering lighting techniques and integrating them effectively into your content creation process, you can elevate your work, attract more subscribers, and foster a loyal community.

Editing and Post-Production Tips

Editing and post-production are critical components of creating high-quality content for your OnlyFans page. The effectiveness of your visuals can significantly impact subscriber engagement and retention. Begin by carefully selecting the software that best suits your needs, whether it's professional-grade options like Adobe Premiere Pro and Final Cut Pro or user-friendly alternatives such as iMovie and Filmora. Familiarize yourself with the basic functionalities, including cutting, color correction, and audio enhancement. Investing time in learning these tools will empower you to present your content in the best possible light, enhancing both your brand and user experience.

When editing, pay close attention to pacing and flow. The rhythm of your content can either captivate or bore your audience. Consider the emotional arc of your videos; a well-paced video can build anticipation and maintain interest. Utilize techniques such as jump cuts to keep the energy high, and don't hesitate to trim unnecessary segments that detract from your core message. Remember that your audience's attention span is limited, so concise and engaging content is vital. Aim for a balance between professionalism and authenticity, allowing your personality to shine through while maintaining a polished look.

Incorporating visual effects and graphics can elevate your content but use them judiciously. Overloading your videos with flashy transitions or excessive overlays can distract from the main message. Instead, focus on subtle enhancements that complement your content. Lower thirds can introduce yourself or highlight key points, while tasteful filters can create a desired mood or aesthetic.

Keep the branding consistent by using the same color palette and fonts across your content. This consistency not only reinforces your identity but also helps in cultivating a recognizable brand that subscribers can connect with.

Sound quality is often overlooked but plays a crucial role in the overall production value of your content. Invest in a good microphone and ensure your audio is clear and balanced. During editing, pay attention to background noise and consider using audio editing software to enhance sound quality. Adding background music can also enhance the viewer's experience, but make sure it aligns with your brand and the tone of your content. Always use royalty-free music or tracks you have rights to, as copyright infringement can lead to significant setbacks in your business.

Finally, never underestimate the power of feedback during the post-production phase. Before releasing your content, consider sharing it with a trusted friend or colleague who can provide constructive criticism. Fresh eyes can often spot issues you've become desensitized to after long editing sessions. Additionally, analyzing viewer metrics once your content goes live will help you understand what resonates with your audience. Use this data to inform future projects, continuously refining your editing and production techniques to better serve your subscribers and enhance your OnlyFans business.

10

Social Media Integration for Promoting OnlyFans

Choosing the Right Platforms

Choosing the right platforms is a critical step for anyone looking to establish a successful OnlyFans business. With numerous social media networks and content-sharing sites available, it is essential to select those that align with your brand and target audience. Platforms such as Twitter and Instagram have become popular among OnlyFans creators due to their visual nature and ability to engage with potential subscribers. Understanding the demographics and features of each platform will allow you to tailor your content effectively and reach the right audience.

When considering social media platforms, prioritize those that promote adult content or have more lenient policies regarding mature themes. Twitter, for instance, has a vibrant adult content community that allows creators to share teasers, engage with followers, and drive traffic to their OnlyFans page. Similarly, platforms like Reddit have dedicated subreddits for adult content, enabling creators to connect with niche audiences. Identifying and leveraging these spaces can significantly enhance your visibility and subscriber base.

In addition to social media, consider using platforms that facilitate direct communication with your audience. Messaging apps, such as Discord or Telegram, can serve as valuable tools for building an engaged community. These platforms allow for real-time interaction, fostering a sense of intimacy and loyalty among subscribers. By creating exclusive groups or channels, you can share behind-the-scenes content, offer special promotions, and cultivate a more personal relationship with your audience. This engagement can translate into higher retention rates and increased revenue.

Another aspect to consider is the integration of various platforms into your marketing strategy. Use analytics tools to track performance across different channels and measure the effectiveness of your campaigns. This data will help you refine your approach and determine which platforms yield the best results. Additionally, cross-promoting content can amplify your reach; for instance, sharing snippets of your OnlyFans content on Instagram Stories can entice followers to subscribe. Each platform should complement your overall strategy, creating a cohesive brand presence that attracts and retains subscribers.

Finally, always be mindful of the legal considerations and community guidelines associated with each platform. Familiarizing yourself with the regulations regarding adult content will help you avoid potential pitfalls and ensure compliance. Additionally, protecting your personal identity and privacy is crucial, particularly when navigating public platforms. Consider using pseudonyms and separate accounts to maintain anonymity while still promoting your brand effectively. By strategically choosing the right platforms, you can optimize your OnlyFans business and maximize your monetization efforts.

Content Repurposing Strategies

Content repurposing is a vital strategy for OnlyFans models and creators seeking to maximize their reach and efficiency. By taking existing content and adapting it for different platforms or formats, creators can extend the lifespan of their material while minimizing the effort required to produce new content. For instance, a photoshoot intended for an exclusive OnlyFans post can be edited into a series of engaging Instagram stories or posts, allowing creators to attract new subscribers through various channels. This strategy not only diversifies content delivery but also enhances visibility across social media, which is essential for building a larger audience.

One effective approach to content repurposing is to transform longer videos into shorter clips. A comprehensive tutorial or behind-the-scenes video can be broken down into bite-sized snippets suitable for TikTok or Instagram Reels. These short clips can capture attention quickly, drawing followers to the full content available on OnlyFans. This method leverages the growing trend of consuming content in shorter formats, especially among younger audiences. By strategically editing content, creators can generate buzz and entice potential subscribers, leading to increased monetization opportunities.

Additionally, written content can be a powerful tool for repurposing. Blog posts summarizing key themes from exclusive content or detailing personal experiences can be shared on platforms like Medium or personal websites. This not only showcases expertise and personality but also offers a gateway for readers to discover the creator's OnlyFans page. Engaging articles can establish authority within specific niches, helping to attract a dedicated following who may be more inclined to subscribe for exclusive insights and experiences.

Community engagement is another critical aspect of content repurposing. By turning subscriber feedback and interactions into content, creators can foster a deeper connection with their audience. For example, a Q&A session can be recorded and then repurposed into a blog post or a podcast episode. This approach not only highlights the creator's commitment to their community but also provides additional content that appeals to different audience preferences. Engaging with followers' questions and suggestions creates a sense of belonging, encouraging them to remain subscribed and actively participate in the content.

Finally, it is essential to maintain a cohesive brand identity across all repurposed content. This can be achieved through consistent visual styling, tone of voice, and messaging. Whether adapting a video for social media or writing an article for a blog, ensuring that each piece of content aligns with the creator's brand helps to reinforce recognition and trust. By strategically repurposing content while staying true to their identity, OnlyFans models can effectively enhance their marketing strategies, engage their community, and ultimately increase their revenue streams.

Engaging with Followers

Engaging with followers is a crucial aspect of building a successful OnlyFans business. It goes beyond merely posting content; it involves creating a connection that fosters loyalty and encourages subscribers to remain active participants in your community. By understanding your audience and tailoring your interactions to their preferences, you can enhance their experience and drive greater monetization opportunities. This engagement can manifest through personalized messages, exclusive content, and interactive features that make subscribers feel valued and included in your journey.

One effective strategy for engagement is to utilize direct messaging to communicate with your followers. This allows for a more personal touch, enabling you to respond to inquiries, thank subscribers for their support, or provide sneak peeks of upcoming content. Tailoring these messages based on subscriber behavior can significantly increase their sense of belonging. For instance, sending a personalized thank you message to new subscribers not only makes them feel appreciated but also encourages them to explore your content further and share their experiences with others.

Incorporating interactive content such as polls, Q&A sessions, and live streams can also enhance follower engagement. These features invite subscribers to participate actively, enabling them to express their preferences and interests. By consistently involving your audience in content creation decisions, you create a sense of ownership among your followers, which can lead to higher retention rates. Additionally, live interactions allow for real-time feedback and relationship building, further solidifying the bond between you and your audience.

Building an engaged community on OnlyFans also involves leveraging social media platforms to drive conversations and promote your content. Sharing behind-the-scenes glimpses or personal anecdotes on platforms like Twitter or Instagram can pique interest and direct traffic to your OnlyFans page. Engaging with your followers on these platforms helps to establish your personal brand and attracts a wider audience. Always remember to keep your messaging consistent and reflective of your brand identity, ensuring that your online presence resonates with your OnlyFans content.

Finally, consider organizing special events or promotions exclusively for your subscribers to strengthen their loyalty. This could be in the form of limited-time discounts, exclusive content drops, or themed content weeks. Such initiatives create excitement and anticipation, prompting followers to stay engaged and regularly check your page for updates. Building a loyal following takes time and effort, but by actively engaging with your subscribers, you can cultivate a supportive community that not only enhances your OnlyFans experience but also drives your success as a content creator.

11

Managing Finances and Taxes for OnlyFans Income

Tracking Your Income and Expenses

Tracking your income and expenses is a fundamental practice for OnlyFans models and creators looking to build a sustainable business. Keeping detailed records allows you to understand where your money is coming from and where it is going, which is essential for making informed decisions. By categorizing your income from subscriptions, tips, and other revenue streams, as well as your expenses related to content creation, marketing, and platform fees, you can gain clarity on your financial health. This clarity not only aids in budgeting but also enhances your ability to strategize for growth and profitability.

To effectively track your finances, consider utilizing both digital tools and traditional methods. Many creators find success using accounting software or apps designed for small businesses, which can automate much of the process, making it easier to categorize transactions and generate reports. Alternatively, a simple spreadsheet can also suffice for those who prefer a more hands-on approach. Whichever method you choose, consistency is key; regularly updating your records will prevent any financial surprises and provide a clearer picture of your economic landscape.

Understanding the nuances of your income streams is crucial for maximizing earnings. Income can come from various sources, including subscription fees, pay-per-view content, and tips from fans. By analyzing which sources generate the most revenue, you can tailor your content and marketing efforts accordingly. For instance, if you notice that exclusive content generates higher tips, you might want to invest more time in creating that type of material. This type of analysis can lead to not only increased income but also a deeper understanding of your audience's preferences.

On the expense side, it's important to track both fixed and variable costs. Fixed expenses might include platform fees and subscriptions to software or services that enhance your content creation efforts, while variable costs can encompass photography equipment, props, and promotional expenses. By being aware of your spending patterns, you can identify areas where you might cut costs or allocate more resources for better returns. Additionally, documenting your expenses can help during tax season, as many of these costs may be deductible, reducing your overall tax liability.

Finally, maintaining a clear financial overview is essential for long-term success and stability. Regularly reviewing your income and expenses allows you to adjust your strategies and make informed decisions about reinvesting in your business. Whether it's upgrading your equipment, hiring support for marketing, or expanding your content offerings, understanding your financial position will empower you to take calculated risks. Moreover, this practice fosters a sense of professionalism and responsibility, which can enhance your brand's credibility in the competitive landscape of OnlyFans.

Understanding Tax Obligations

Tax obligations are a critical aspect of running an OnlyFans business that every content creator must understand. As an OnlyFans model or creator, the income you earn is subject to taxation, just like any other form of income. It is essential to recognize that being self-employed or running a side hustle comes with unique tax responsibilities. This subchapter will shed light on how to navigate these obligations effectively, ensuring compliance while maximizing your financial returns.

First and foremost, it is vital to determine your tax classification. Most OnlyFans creators operate as sole proprietors, meaning their business income is reported on their personal tax return. Understanding this classification helps you prepare for the types of taxes you will owe, including income tax and self-employment tax. Familiarize yourself with the tax rates in your jurisdiction, as they can vary significantly. Keeping accurate records of your earnings and expenses will streamline the filing process and help you avoid potential penalties.

Additionally, it is advisable to set aside a portion of your income for taxes. A common rule of thumb is to reserve around 20-30% of your earnings to cover your tax obligations. This practice not only prevents last-minute financial stress when tax season arrives but also allows you to approach your tax responsibilities proactively. Consider opening a separate savings account specifically for taxes to help you manage these funds effectively throughout the year.

Another essential aspect of managing your tax obligations is understanding deductible expenses. As an OnlyFans creator, you can deduct various business-related expenses, such as equipment, software, marketing costs, and even a portion of your internet and home office expenses. Keeping detailed records and receipts of these expenses can significantly reduce your taxable income, maximizing your overall profit. Consulting with a tax professional who understands the unique landscape of online content creation can also provide tailored advice on maximizing your deductions.

Lastly, staying informed about local and federal tax laws is crucial. Tax regulations can change, and new guidelines specific to online businesses may emerge. Regularly reviewing tax updates and seeking professional guidance can help you remain compliant and avoid surprises. By understanding your tax obligations and implementing sound financial practices, you position yourself for long-term success in your OnlyFans journey while ensuring that your hard-earned income is managed wisely.

Financial Planning for Growth

Financial planning is a crucial aspect of running a successful OnlyFans business. For creators looking to maximize their income and ensure sustainable growth, a well-structured financial plan serves as the foundation for long-term success. It is essential to not only track income from subscriptions but also to explore diversified monetization methods. By understanding the intricacies of budgeting, saving, and investing, you can better position your OnlyFans venture as a profitable and potentially life-changing endeavor.

To begin, establishing a clear budget is vital. This budget should account for all sources of income, including subscriptions, tips, pay-per-view content, and any additional revenue streams you may implement. Allocate funds for essential expenses such as content creation tools, marketing efforts, and any associated fees with the OnlyFans platform. A thorough understanding of your cash flow will enable you to identify areas where you can cut costs or reinvest for growth. Regularly reviewing and adjusting your budget will keep your financial plan aligned with your evolving goals.

In addition to budgeting, it is important to set aside a portion of your income for taxes. Many creators underestimate their tax obligations, which can lead to significant financial stress down the line. By saving a percentage of your earnings each month, you will be better prepared for tax season and avoid any surprises that could disrupt your financial stability. Consulting with a tax professional familiar with the unique circumstances of OnlyFans creators can provide valuable insights into deductions and strategies to minimize your tax burden.

Investing in your business is another critical component of financial planning for growth. Reinvesting profits into high-quality photography, videography, or marketing can lead to enhanced content, which may attract a larger audience and increase subscriber numbers. Additionally, consider investing in tools or platforms that streamline your workflow or enhance your engagement with fans. The goal is to create a virtuous cycle where reinvested income generates more significant returns, ultimately boosting your overall profitability.

Lastly, building an engaged community is an integral part of financial success on OnlyFans. Fostering relationships with your subscribers and creating a loyal fan base can lead to higher retention rates and increased spending. Employing marketing techniques, such as personalized content or exclusive offers, can enhance subscriber interaction and drive more significant revenue. By focusing on community building and maintaining a strong brand identity, you will not only increase your income but also create a sustainable and fulfilling business model that thrives in the competitive landscape of content creation.

www.ingramcontent.com/pod-product-compliance
Lightning Source LLC
Chambersburg PA
CBHW071336140726
47996CB00005B/1997